Container Gardening For Beginners:

Essential Guide on How to Grow and Harvest Plants, Vegetables and Fruits in Tubs, Pots and Other Containers

By

Erin Morrow

Table of Contents

Introduction 5

Chapter 1. Container Gardening Benefits 6

Chapter 2. Starting Your Container Garden 9

Chapter 3. Basic Steps 12

Chapter 4. Fertilizing is Key 17

Chapter 5. Load The Container Properly 20

Chapter 6. What to Grow 22

Chapter 7. Helpful Tips 27

Thank You Page 31

Container Gardening For Beginners: Essential Guide on How to Grow and Harvest Plants, Vegetables and Fruits in Tubs, Pots and Other Containers

By Erin Morrow

© Copyright 2015 Erin Morrow

Reproduction or translation of any part of this work beyond that permitted by section 107 or 108 of the 1976 United States Copyright Act without permission of the copyright owner is unlawful. Requests for permission or further information should be addressed to the author.

This publication is designed to provide accurate and authoritative information in regard to the subject matter covered. This work is sold with the understanding that the publisher is not engaged in rendering legal, accounting, or other professional services. If legal advice or other expert assistance is required, the services of a competent professional person should be sought.

First Published, 2015

Printed in the United States of America

Introduction

Gardening is said to be one of the most therapeutic hobbies you can engage yourself in, whether you have a green thumb or not. It is said to be not only a good exercise for the body, but also a good source of sense of fulfillment, a good relaxing technique, and obviously, an opportunity to contribute in your own little way, to advocate the importance of nature.

There are several types of gardening. Categorized according to direction of growth, you have vertical and horizontal gardening. Categorized according to the type of plants, there are vegetable, fruit, ornamental gardening types, among so many others. Gardening is also classified based on where to plant your crops; the ground, the bed and the container. These varied ways of gardening may overlap with each other, but one of the most common, convenient and recommended type of gardening is that which makes use of containers. This is because of numerous reasons.

Chapter 1. Container Gardening Benefits

To help you get motivated to start gardening, here are some reasons to garden using containers.

It is the easiest form of gardening. If there is one type of gardening that can be best recommended for beginners, that's container gardening. Even at a young age, kids can be enabled to start appreciating nature through plants, if given the chance to plant in a container. If kids can do it, adults can most likely become excellent in doing it as well. Creating a container garden can be argued to be achieved easiest and fastest, that all you need are the usual seeds (or plants), the appropriate soil, and the container.

Its portability feature is superb. You can grow your plants anywhere you want if you are using containers, as long as there is adequate sunlight (or its alternative) for it, along with water. The very good advantage of planting in containers is that you can transfer your plants nearly wherever you want to keep them. It is good for people who love rearranging the house or the front yard, who love variation in the layout of what he or she sees.

It has the capability to adjust. Plants have preferences too. There are plants that grow well in one part of the earth, while others prefer to say small in another. Bonsai plants usually grow in high altitudes for instance. But by using containers you can bring them to your living room and maintain them wherever you want to as long as you control the environment in which you place them. It is a matter of milieu modification to make things work. This is the power of portability.

It could be cheap. You might be thinking that with the requirement of a container in container gardening, there is an additional cost, compared to just planting the seeds at the backyard. Not. Containers may be chosen to be in pricey forms, but this is just an add-on. A container can be anything you do not even have to buy. You can utilize an old jar or bucket, an unused bin or tub – just anything that you can fit your soil in, after putting some drainage holes under it. If you want some aesthetic effect, you need not go expensive either. You can just rely on your creative juices, and anything goes for your beautification pleasure.

It can accommodate almost any plant you want. It is believed that there is almost no plant you want reasonably, that cannot be grown in a container garden. You can grow vegetables, ornamental plants, herbs, or even trees – of various sizes, to make it even more interesting.

It can make you think of so many other beautiful things about it that this list will never stop growing in length.

Chapter 2. Starting Your Container Garden

If you think this is about to be your first time to do container gardening, you might have to think again and harder until you get to that point of your memory when somebody either from home or from school, assisted you in planting certain seeds in a small, improvised container so you can watch it develop. Maybe it is when you first experimented with your childhood friend, or on your own on what would happen if you soaked those beans overnight, or longer. You probably even had an attempt to 're-plant' a flower on a vase and see how long it would stay as fresh, or if it would grow any further.

Of course, not everything written on the preceding paragraph can be strictly considered as 'gardening', but this is only to show that there have been attempts on your part in the earlier times of your life, consciously or otherwise, to grow something. This shows that naturally, there has always been that interest inside you to do this. You may not view yourself as a green thumb alright, but as long as the drive is there, your gardening experience will surely bring you pleasure.

The elements

In starting with container gardening, it is important to consider the different elements involved in this kind of gardening. These include light, soil, fertilizer, container and plants. Light is nearly any plant needs. Most herbs are said to need full sun at around 6 hours in one day. It does not however help that the sun is in its scorching state, but in cases like this, just have your container gardens saved.

There are different kinds of soil, with different characteristics. In container gardening, there is what is called potting soil which provides good drainage to most of your herbs. Drainage holes in the container are also essential in order to allow your plants' roots to breathe. Fertilizers are said to be optional, especially with herbs. Some herbs are better grown alone, without much water or fertilizers, or attention. Whichever your pick is, just remember not to over-fertilize herbs.

The container is another big thing that matters in this kind of gathering. In fact, it is what defines this kind. While you can choose anything to serve as an herb container, the size of the container requires quite your knowledge of your plants' needs. Keep in mind that the smaller the container, the less soil there is. To address possible problems on your inability to attend to your plants in a daily basis, there is what is called self-watering containers. What this kind of container provides is a constant level on their moisture on the soil. However, unlike herbs like chives, mint and parsley, other herbs prefer some dry times, thus would not be a good candidate for the use of this kind of container.

Chapter 3. Basic Steps

For further details on starting your container garden, here's a step-by-step guide specifically, with kitchen-friendly plants, as examples.

Decide on what you would like to (and can actually) grow.

In choosing what to grow, you must specifically consider your time, your lifestyle and your needs, as these define the extent of commitment you can give your garden. For example, if you want your pots to be decorative In that case, you pick ornamental plants. However, if your idea of a hobby is simple being happy-go-lucky, with no commitments, just come and go, it's either you think it all over again, or choose low maintenance plants to grow in your pots. In this way, you only have to water them once in a while.

Many container gardening enthusiasts choose growing what they need in the kitchen. Also, several of the kitchen experts are now growing their herbs in their very working area. This is probably a good way to combine your passion with your work towards pleasurable functionality. For these people, good and common options for container gardening include certain herbs, lettuce and tomatoes – different variants of such, that is.

Situate your plants in a strategic manner.

Being strategic allows you to implementing a useful way to achieve a predetermined plan, or more. This can happen whether you want your ornaments in the living room, or your insect repellants in the outdoors; whether you want your air freshening greens in the toilet, or yes, your beautifying robust herbs in the kitchen, you are being strategic, wise, and indeed, cool.

As mentioned earlier, light is a major element in gardening. Herbs, at the most, need full sun, and so a strategic spot for your herbs and vegetables must be established where sunlight is abundant, being careful not to dehydrate your plants. Further, if there are other considerations you wish to include in terms of the decision on where to place your beauties, feel free to incorporate them.

Choose the details of your container.

Things to consider in choosing or making your containers depend largely on your choices of plants to grow. Do their roots need extra space underneath the soil surface? Are you going for taller types of plants that might need a wider base for support? Do you intend to go for uniformity, instead of being creative with just any seeming rubbish there is at the basement? These among many, are factors that may affect the functionality of your containers.

In case you would like to grow herbs and lettuce, you will be needing a shallow container with a large surface area and a bottom that allows the roots to aerate – that is a screened one. If you would like to grow tomatoes, a bucket, or any deeper container will do the trick.

Simply, the containers you should pick, in order for the plants to achieve their fullest vibrancy, should provide adequate space for roots and soil media, in order for the plant to thrive. Your functional 'pots', which will contain your exuberant plants, may be used in or around your house or office to provide focal points, serve as dividers, secure privacy, screen objectionable views, and grow your edible garden.

Moreover, whether to purchase or to build your container will depend largely on how you may want to present your garden. But aesthetics does not exclusively dictate that you have to purchase your container. For many, finding whatever is available around is as much fun as choosing among rows of commercially made pots . You may plant in an old toy bin, a tub, or even a boot, depending on how you interpret beauty and functionality.

The types of containers you choose will make a significant difference in how frequently you should be able to water your plant. If you are using a plastic pot, know that plastic does not absorb water; it holds it. Clay pots, on the other hand, are what absorb water, so plants will need to be watered more frequently when using thing kind of container. Glazed pots are somewhere in between plastic and clay pots, in that they do hold some water, but still absorb moisture.

Chapter 4. Fertilizing is Key

Fertilizers are needed in keeping the soil able to nourish your plants, thus are always part of your gardening essentials. Fertilizing is critical in maintaining the level of organic matter in the soil, from where your plants grow, which cannot go too low on the nutrients.

Incorporating fertilizers in non-container gardening is usually done when tilling the soil. This is done in anticipation of the soil's depleting organic material, as the more voracious plants consume its supply. This is not exactly needed in container gardening, as the fertilizer may be built into the soil from the start. However, for heavy-feeding plants like squash and certain tomatoes, supplemental fertilizers are still needed. Although different vegetable types require varied fertilization requirements, you may apply the following basic guidelines to most of the veggies you would like to grow in your containers. But first, prepare your bucket, potting soil, slow-release fertilizer, and water-soluble fertilizer.

First, fill your chosen container with the appropriate soil, after which, pour a small amount of water – just enough to allow moisture after mixing it with your hands. Next, measure half a tablespoon of a balanced fertilizer that is labeled slow-release, and incorporate it to the soil, per gallon. Mix the proportion of fertilizer to the soil until evenly distributed. Next, fill the containers with the mixture before transplanting the vegetables into the filled pots.

Halfway during the growing season, you may apply soluble fertilizer, which you diluted in water, while carefully following instructions on its label. You may do this for the remaining period of the growing season, by watering the plants with the solution every one or two weeks.

Another thing to consider in fertilizing is the need of developing vegetable plants to be grown organically, that is, with the supplementation of organic fertilizers. The other good things about organic fertilizing are that they could be cheap, and that they have long-term and stable effects on the soil, as opposed to the synthetic type of fertilizers. Such steady longer effects make it even more suitable for container gardening, as you will not likely have to till the soil as you are to do that in ground gardening.

Chapter 5. Load The Container Properly

When filling in container, compost soil is placed at a height of two to four inches. If you are planting sprouts, then you should give them a few inches of space around the roots. However, scattering the seeds even across the platter will do the job if you are planting seeds. One suggestion to be more practical with growing herbs is to keep two or three containers of each plant going at once, so that when you've clipped one plant, you have another one ready for your next meal.

If you are considering grouping various plants in one container, remember that the plants have the same needs on the amount of water. Therefore, they must be planted in such a way that their roots are not on the same levels, and that those that should be driest are closest to the surface.

From here, you may give yourself a pat on the back. You now know the basics of starting with your container garden! How exciting could it be to do the things needed in order to maintain them? You know it does not end with scattering the seeds, or implanted sprouts. You still have some remaining things to do to witness the amazing development of your plants, and to eventually harvest what is yours! For such, consider what follow.

Consistently water your plants regularly. Damp soil is what herbs should be grown from. Frying them out will render them unhealthy. Your intake of anything unhealthy can also yield to unhealthy results on your body. Tomatoes, however, are easy to over-water. So before watering them you should check the soil. If the soil is moist, then wait till the moment when it becomes dry and only then water. It is best to water around the base of the plant, rather than through the leaves.

When it is time to harvest from your plants, you would want use the apt scissors to snip the leaves or vegetables. In order for you to do this, clip the leaves around the base of the plant first, so that it will continue to grow and fill out. You may now enjoy the freshest herbs you could ever get, and that is straight from your very own container garden. Rewarding as it sounds, it would feel better in reality.

Chapter 6. What to Grow

Tomatoes. As always, the right container size is crucial in growing tomatoes. So is such consideration essential in growing different variants. To grow the smaller variants of tomatoes, containers with around 6-liter capacity at the least are advisable, while for the larger ones, a minimum capacity of 10 liters should be used for one. A high recommendation is given by experts on growing cherry tomatoes instead of the big ones, as they more easily grow and ripen, giving you the best of what you may need from the crop. Varieties of vince cherry tomato you might want to include are black cherry, gardener's delight, sungold, and sun cherry premium, while some examples of dwarf bush ones are minibel, micro tom, tom thumb, balcony red, and balcony yellow.

When preparing the pot and the soil, remember that the roots of tomato plants need to breathe. To facilitate this, you may add around 15% of perlite in your growing mix. Also, you may create small holes on the sides of the pot so that the roots receive sufficient supply of air. Aside from holes on the container, support may also be provided for bush tomatoes with the use of stake or strings. Watering technique is also important. What to keep in mind is to saturate the entire area of soil you can see; otherwise, you are merely wetting the topmost layer. Other than watering, an important way to keep the tomatoes growing, is feeding it with tomato feed. You may dilute the tomato feed with double the amount of the recommended water, so you can distribute the feeding into an increase frequency, and less quantity in each feeding.

Herbs. Herbs are preferred by many to be grown in containers, not only because they look stunning in those pots, and they are easy to access and move when cooking, but also because they are much easier to manage and to make the most out of when they are grown there. Examples of herb that can be grown in pots or similar containers are Nasturtium, forest green parsley, Genovese basil, lemon balm, and lemon thyme.

Alaska nasturtium is one of the attractive ones of its kind, not only for its appearance, but also for the awesome flavor it adds to food. Its seeds are best sown outdoors when the weather is warm, usually in late spring. Fertilizing it is hardly encouraged; instead, perlite is incorporated to the plant in order to elicit the growth of its flowers more than leaves. Cutting the plant is as essential as spraying it with a pyrethrum-based organic pesticide in late summer, in order to get rid of aphids.

Forest green parsley is one of the herbs that are most frequently used in the kitchen, as it can be incorporated in many recipes. To grow it, you may do so through means of seed germination. Seeds are soaked in warm water for the first two days and left indoor within an average of 11 weeks before the last frost. Before planting the seeds, they should be rinsed after changing the water once. Cover the seeds with moist, well-drained soil, and keep from sunlight. Parsley plants are cut occasionally and fertilized to keep their robustness throughout the entire season.

Genovese basil is called the 'queen of the herb garden', a herbal plant that is said to be easy to grow. Its seeds are sown indoors at around five weeks before the last frost. Heat leads to the flowering of this type of basil, so if you want to keep them bushy. Further, if you want further leaf production, usually for consumption, it helps if you cutting back stems.

Lemon balm, a lemon-scented herb is a fast growing plant, is best grown in a container, as it could overtake whatever space is reserved for it. In growing this mildly sedative herb, seeds are sown indoors for six weeks before last frost, and are lightly covered with average, full-drained soil. To keep them bushy, you may cut plants during the growing season to provide your kitchen with fresh foliage for different recipes.

Lemon thyme, known for its intense lemon aroma, is best grown in full sun within average-well drain soil. Similarly with lemon balm, this herb could appear rather messy on the ground, so is best to be grown inside a nice container, from plants, and not seeds. Lemon thyme must hibernate outdoors, and be trimmed back to its livelier form during spring. You may cut back its stems to trim during the growing season.

Generally, in harvesting herbs, as the rule goes, the more you pick, the more you'll get. When you keep pinching most of those healthy plants, you help them become bushier, thus prettier.

Chapter 7. Helpful Tips

Now if you are deciding to grab some pots and selecting some seeds and plants and soil, it is also important that you know some dos and don'ts, which can help you enjoy your experience in container gardening. Others have made the mistakes; you cannot afford to repeat them. Others have paved the way to your success; learn from them.

Plants drown too; keep them safe. Water is good for plants; that's a fact. Water is good for you too; in fact, it is a necessity. But hyperhidrosis is something you do not wish for yourself. While you are trying to keep yourself hydrated, you only do so in moderation. Your plants can drown too. If you over-water your plants, their green leaves may fade to yellow, and your plant turn weak. Before this could even happen, pay attention to your soil; it may be too wet. In this case, adjust by transferring the container to a spot where the soil can dry a bit, just enough not to completely dry them out.

Moderation is key; know how much you should water. Different plants have relatively different needs. When choosing your plants, know how much watering they need, as not only do you want to keep them from drowning, you also want them to avoid getting dehydrated. In order for you to know that you are watering enough, make sure you see the water above the surface of the soil, and not merely allowing the former to just wet the latter at the topmost layer.

Keep your garden disease-free. When buying plants, stay away from those that need resuscitation. Choose the healthy ones. When some parts of your plant fall off, make sure to take them out if it does not qualify as compost. It may infect the entire plant/plants in case you mistakenly commit this. Also, keep your plants away from weeds, pests and animals. Although you grow your plants in containers, there are still chances for your plants to experience this, so just in case you see some little crawling beings, simply yank it off to keep your garden clean and nice.

Stay away from frustration. Consider your lifestyle when planning to start maintaining container gardens.

Is this something you can put your commitment on? Do you have time for it? Think of this endeavor as a commitment. Can you manage to keep up with it possible demands this may ask of you? In cases where you need to leave without prior notice do you have a plan of action while you are away? In case you travel a lot, and leave the house most often than not, there are solutions to your dilemma.

First, you may either go for an automatic drip irrigation system. Drip irrigation is said to be the most effective method of irrigating, much more than sprinklers. This drip system is said to be very convenient because it not only wastes much less water, it is also said to be easy to install, easy to design, and able to reduce disease of plants brought about by a certain level of moisture of the soil. The mechanism of this type of irrigation lies on that the water soaks directly into the soil prior to it can run off or evaporate. Another mechanism showing its efficacy is that the water is applied only when needed, rather than spread everywhere. Perfect for your potential away-from-home concern.

The second option to solve your problem in case you cannot be home to water your plants is the use of self-watering containers that are self-watering. Self-watering or sub-irrigation is said to be a method of irrigating your plants in which the water is accessed from the bottom, allowing the water to soak upwards towards the plant through what referred to as called capillary action.

These solutions, especially the second one, are actually feasible approaches, but in case they seem to be too expensive for you or not doable for you, you can always choose plants that do not need as much water to survive. It's your choice.

Thank You Page

I want to personally thank you for reading my book. I hope you found information in this book useful and I would be very grateful if you could leave your honest review about this book. I certainly want to thank you in advance for doing this.

If you have the time, you can check my other books too.

www.ingramcontent.com/pod-product-compliance
Lightning Source LLC
LaVergne TN
LVHW021746060526
838200LV00052B/3506